THE TEMPERATE HOUSE
at the Royal Botanic Gardens, Kew

CONTENTS

KEW'S TEMPERATE HOUSE

Kew's Grade I listed Temperate House is the world's largest surviving Victorian-era glasshouse; its reopening in May 2018 marked its 155th anniversary. It is home to Kew's temperate zone plants, containing specimens from South Africa, the Americas, Asia, Australia, New Zealand and oceanic islands. Some of its best known species, such as its tree ferns, have been in Kew's collection since the glasshouse first opened, or even longer.

Initiated by Kew's first director William Jackson Hooker during a period of great change both at Kew and in the wider world, the Temperate House was the last of Hooker's great projects. Construction began in 1859 — the same year Darwin's *On the Origin of Species* was published — and the house opened (incomplete) in 1863. By the time the final wing opened in 1899 William Thiselton-Dyer was director and Kew's role in imperial botany — supplying, receiving and in all ways supporting the transfer of plants across the Empire — was at its apex. The Temperate House was arguably the clearest public manifestation of this work, being filled with economically important plants such as the quinine tree (*Cinchona officinalis*), historically used to treat malaria, and tea (*Camellia sinensis*), and showcasing flora from some of the Empire's most important colonies including Australia, New Zealand and the Cape in South Africa. By the 1970s, when the glasshouse closed for its first major restoration, Kew's work was shifting in line with the growing global awareness of the often-unintended consequences of humanity's actions on the planet, for example by becoming the UK's Scientific Authority (for flora) for CITES, the international convention established in 1976 that protects species by regulating international trade.

Today, Kew is a key partner of global conservation organisations and the Temperate House collection is significant for the rare plants it safeguards, including threatened endemic species (those unique to a particular location) and some species that are now extinct in the wild. These plants play an important role in Kew's scientific research and work in conservation and habitat restoration across many parts of the world.

THE TEMPERATE CLIMATE ZONE AND BIODIVERSITY HOTSPOTS

The temperate climate zone falls between the tropics and polar regions, covering 40% of Earth's land surface, and experiences moderate temperatures with clearly defined seasons. Temperate areas also exist at higher elevations within areas generally considered tropical. The climate zones represented in the Temperate House include several global biodiversity hotspots — key areas of plant diversity. Thirty-five biodiversity hotspots have been defined, together they cover just 2.3% of the Earth's land surface but are home to 50% of all endemic plant species.

The newly restored Temperate House contains over 10,000 plants from 1,500 species, including some of the world's rarest.

A NEW GLASSHOUSE FOR KEW

The birth of a national garden

Kew had reached a low point by the late 1830s. For almost 20 years the Gardens had languished in neglect following the deaths of King George III and his botanical adviser, Kew's caretaker and champion, Joseph Banks. By 1838 dismemberment was threatened and their fate rested on the report of a Treasury-appointed Committee, headed by Dr Lindley, respected botanist and Secretary of the Horticultural Society (now RHS). His findings and proposals did more than ensure Kew's survival — they provided a blueprint to turn Kew from a royal garden into a government-sponsored national garden.

Lindley's vision for this 'national garden' befitted the era's imperialist mindset. He saw Kew becoming the central node in a network of smaller gardens spanning the Empire which, under its control, could 'supply the mother country in every thing that is useful in the vegetable kingdom', and through which Kew could source 'authentic and official information on points connected with the establishment of new colonies.' Two fundamental changes were required for this to become reality. First, responsibility for the Gardens needed to rest with government rather than the Crown. This transfer occurred in 1840. Second, a talented, dedicated leader was needed, one capable of implementing rapid change.

William Jackson Hooker took the post of director in 1841 and during his 24 years in charge the Gardens were transformed. The grounds were enlarged and united in a landscape plan designed by William Andrews Nesfield and opening hours were extended. Visitor numbers soared, many arriving through the new Main Gate designed by Decimus Burton and erected in 1846.

The policy of sending plant collectors overseas, originally initiated by Banks, was revived in 1843. A surge of new introductions followed, but the plant-traffic was not at all one-way as Kew freely supplied colonial governors, directors of gardens and other officials with plants for food and industry. This global plant transfer was made possible by the invention of the Wardian case (a mini transportable greenhouse). Kew was an early adopter, and by 1847 they were in regular use. In 1851 Hooker wrote that during the past 15 years the cases had been responsible for 'introducing more new and valuable plants to our gardens than were imported during the preceding century'.

left: The Temperate House in 1890, before the addition of the end wings.

Temperate House, c. 1905.

This swell in live plant collections put further strain on Kew's already overcrowded glasshouses, described in Lindley's report as consisting of 'ten different stoves and greenhouses ... crowded together without plan or arrangement'. Hooker earmarked the most dilapidated for demolition and wasted no time finding alternative provision. Citrus trees were removed from the Orangery in 1841 so it could be used for large greenhouse specimens, and the 'Architectural Greenhouse' (Nash Conservatory) was pressed into use as a stove for palms and other tropical specimens. These were only ever intended as temporary measures. In 1844 Burton was commissioned to design a suitable hothouse. In what effectively became a collaboration with structural engineer and iron-founder Richard Turner, the elegant curvilinear Palm House was erected, opening in 1848 to great acclaim.

DECIMUS BURTON AND WILLIAM CUBBITT

Architect Decimus Burton (1800–1881) was a leading exponent of the Greek revival style, arguably best known for his work in London parks, including Hyde Park Screen. His collaboration with Joseph Paxton on the famous Great Stove at Chatsworth blew up into a public spat over who had been responsible for the design. Burton was significant to Kew's transformation under William Hooker, designing the Main Gate (1846) and Museum No. 1 (1856) in addition to the iconic Palm House (1844–8) and the Temperate House (1859–62).

William Cubitt and Co. was a major London contracting firm and civil engineering contractors, with works including the original Euston Station, the Bank of England and extensions to the National Gallery. Cubitt (1791–1863) was also a politician, serving as MP for Andover and Lord Mayor of London.

Campaign for a new conservatory

Kew's tropical collection now had a suitable home but the same could not be said for its semi-hardy plants, still scattered across the grounds in inappropriate buildings. Hooker first stated the need for a purpose-built temperate house in Kew's 1853 annual report. In 1855 he reported that many temperate plants 'once the pride of these Gardens' were 'suffering beyond recovery for want of suitable winter shelter', and that a new glasshouse was 'an imperative necessity if the remnant of these splendid specimens is to be saved.' Each year he upped the pressure, in 1856 stating that one of the old greenhouses had been demolished in anticipation of a new conservatory being built. By 1857 he wrote that Kew's famous collection of temperate plants must be spoken about 'almost in the past tense.' Kew's transformation, he argued, would not be complete until the temperate plants were properly housed:

> 'What is really required to render the gardens complete is, as much accommodation for the large trees and shrubs of temperate climates as was granted for tropical plants 12 years ago in the erection of our noble Palm House ... then, and not till then, we shall have attained to all that this great national establishment ought to be.'

The Gardeners Chronicle drew attention to the cause in January 1858. It reported that the question had been raised in Parliament during the debate on Civil Service Estimates for 1856 but the response had been negative and for the next two years, despite Hooker's mounting pressure, Parliament had not returned to the issue.

This sympathetic coverage may have steeled Hooker's nerve, for soon afterwards he sent his initial requirements to the First Commissioner of Works. These emphasised economy, stating that the house would be cheaper to construct than the Palm House, partly due to the abolishment of glass duty, but mostly through utilising a simpler design and cheaper materials.

Temperate House central block, view from the gallery.

The Commissioner at last agreed that provision would be made the following year, and Burton was commissioned to draw up plans and estimates.

The estimate (c.£25,000–30,000) was put before Parliament in the summer of 1859. During the debate one influential member, Joseph Paxton, opposed the cost, stating his belief that the house could be built for £10,000, and using the same speech to question whether Hooker was turning Kew into 'a gaudy flower garden'. A later comment suggests this intervention may have been prompted less out of concern for the public purse than by worry about competition for his own Crystal Palace, then run as a private venture. 'Every man in the country,' he said, 'would wish to see Kew kept up; it ought to be kept up as a beautiful garden, but it ought not to be decorated at the public expense so as to compete with places which were established on commercial principles.' Whatever the motive, his objection carried weight and the Treasury only sanctioned £10,000 for Kew's new glasshouse.

Design and construction

Plans were refined throughout 1859 and by December Burton had produced many finely detailed drawings. Broadly these were in line with Hooker's original brief for a central glazed parallelogram with a straight sloping roof, large windows that could be opened for ample ventilation and easily-repairable timber sashes. Burton's design incorporated two wings at either end, capable of being added at any time and accessed through interlinking octagons. A maximum height of 60 ft rather than the 50 ft initially suggested by Hooker was settled upon, and although Hooker had been prepared to do without one, provision was made for a gallery with two spiral staircases. The designs included ideas for the decorative urns and statues of Flora and Sylvanus. For Burton the decorative elements, the focal point of the exterior, were integral to the whole. In the end, due to the financial constraints, ornamentation was only added to the eastern façade.

The building contract went to William Cubitt & Co. Using gravel and sand excavated from the recently developed Lake, a raised geometric terrace mirroring the building's footprint (including the wings) was created. The two octagons were erected first followed by the central parallelogram, which was completed in 1862. This exhausted the Treasury funds and so the wings were not built, despite their foundations having been partially laid and some ironwork made.

The Temperate House opened to the public in May 1863. Hooker, much aggrieved at its unfinished state, complained to the Board of Works that its incompleteness was an 'eyesore' that rendered his plans for a large display of colonial plants an impossibility. 'In the natural course of events,' his memo concluded, 'I shall not again be entrusted with so important an undertaking'. Two years later, in 1865, he died, with his last grand project — the finale of his transformation of Kew — still incomplete.

CHOOSING A LOCATION

Hooker chose to site the new conservatory in his new Arboretum. Its prominence on Pagoda Vista visually links the Pagoda to the Palm House, although his son Joseph Dalton Hooker later wrote he thought its site was too close to the Vista and that its precise position was chosen to avoid felling some of the Arboretum's finest trees. From today's perspective it seems a little tucked away — but had Kew Gardens station been built where originally planned, matters would have been very different. In anticipation of the station ornate cast iron carriage gates were erected opposite the Temperate House on Kew Road in 1868, to form the principle entrance for visitors arriving by train. However, the station was eventually sited half a mile down the road. Despite public demand the gates, known as The Queen's Gate, were never opened and in 1889 they were re-erected in alignment with the station and renamed Victoria Gate.

Temperate House doorway,
c.1900–1910.

THE TEMPERATE HOUSE'S EARLY YEARS

The Temperate House opened, displaying plants from Australia, New Zealand, Asia, Africa, Central and South America, some Pacific Islands and southern Europe. The central block was laid out in 20 beds: 10 in the northern half and 10 in the southern half, each separated by a gravel path and with small specimens placed on perimeter benches. Australian *Banksia*, *Acacia* and *Eucalyptus* were scattered through the beds, excluding beds 10 and 17 which were reserved for Himalayan rhododendrons. The majority of large specimens had been moved from the Architectural Greenhouse (Nash Conservatory) and Orangery; the latter was then converted to a wood museum and opened to the public. The northern octagon mainly contained Australian, New Zealand and South African Cape shrubs transferred from Chambers's Great Stove, finally freeing it for demolition, while the southern octagon was filled with species and cultivated varieties of citrus fruits. During the summer plants in the octagons were moved onto the terrace.

Organisation of the collection did not change substantially until the wings were added in the late 1890s. A review from *Garden and Forest* in 1892 praised the plants natural arrangement and generally robust health, listing the star attractions as 'tree ferns, palms, acacias, Sikkim rhododendrons, camellias, araucarias and dammaras' and noting that large specimens were best viewed from the gallery. William Dallimore, recently apprenticed to Kew as a gardener, remarked in his unpublished memoir that when he first saw the Temperate House in 1891, the scenes from this gallery filled him with wonder.

Five years after his arrival, Dallimore had risen through the ranks to take charge of the Temperate House. The plant collection was no longer so robust; on the contrary its condition was a grave concern and Dallimore's primary task was to restore it to health. Tree ferns, one of the house's chief features, were suffering badly, their young fronds badly deformed and some dead. Rhododendrons, acacias and camellias were also in decline, and insect pests were increasing rapidly.

This sorry state was largely the result of placing together plants with opposing needs. Since 1891 plants had been moved to the Temperate House from the overcrowded Palm House. These semi-tropical new arrivals required a warmer and closer atmosphere than, for example, rhododendrons or camellias, which need little heat and plenty of ventilation to thrive. Dallimore set about reconditioning the House, aerating the main beds and fumigating with nicotine. These measures helped, but what the collection really needed to thrive was the long-awaited wings, which would allow the plants to be housed according to their climatic needs. Luckily, by this stage Thiselton-Dyer had — after several years of pressuring — secured funds for the erection of the wings. It would not be long before Dallimore faced another major task: reorganising the plant collection of the world's largest glasshouse.

'Vegetation of Australia and New Zealand as represented in the Temperate House of the Royal Gardens, Kew', from *Gardeners' Magazine* 22nd December 1888.

AN ARCHITECTURAL WONDER COMPLETE

Thiselton-Dyer's 'chronic eyesore'

With the Temperate House open little was done to ensure its completion during Joseph Dalton Hooker's directorship; it was his successor William Thiselton-Dyer who took up the cause in 1891. The following year, when *Garden and Forest* published a review praising the glasshouse as 'one of the largest and handsomest plant structures in Europe' but noting that 'only a portion of the original design has been carried out,' Thiselton-Dyer saw an opportunity. He sent the review to the Office of Works along with a memo bemoaning the 'chronic eyesore' that was the incomplete Temperate House.

In 1894, the First Commissioner finally prepared a statement for the Treasury only for it to be struck out by the Chancellor, who commented that 'a nation that requires a fleet, must do without a greenhouse.' At this, the prominent politician Joseph Chamberlain, who had already been advocating for Kew behind the scenes, appealed to the Chancellor personally and secured £6,000 for the erection of one wing — a sum £1,000 less than the original estimated cost over 30 years earlier. To progress matters beyond this took a further two interventions in 1895 from Chamberlain, now Secretary of State for the Colonies, plus an angry memo from Thiselton-Dyer to the Board of Works in January 1896 enumerating every delay over the past five years.

The south wing was finally erected later that year using iron columns with wooden sashes and frames. The construction was completed by the successful glasshouse manufacturers Mackenzie and Moncur, the original contractor declaring bankruptcy partway through the project. After this protracted battle, authorisation for the north wing followed relatively swiftly in early 1897.

The Mexican and Himalaya Houses

The south wing opened in July 1897. Its then name, the Mexican House, did not indicate the plants geographic origin so much as the temperature range they required, a range warmer than the central block but cooler than the Palm House. Writing about the Mexican House in his 1908 book on Kew, William Jackson Bean singled out for praise two groups of succulent plants growing on rockwork, along with fine South African euphorbias and strelitzias, and Javanese rhododendrons.

The north wing, then called the Himalaya House, was kept cooler than the central block and housed mostly north Asian vegetation. It opened in May 1899 with rhododendron species, varieties and hybrids as the stars of the house. Dallimore recalled a trainload of rhododendrons being delivered from a nursery near Falmouth, to supplement those moved from the central block.

Illustration showing end wings complete, c.1900.

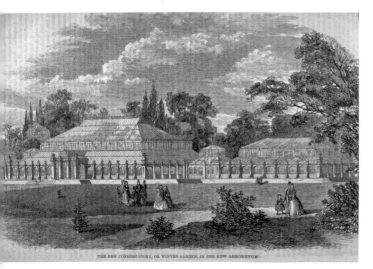

THE NEW CONSERVATORY, OR WINTER GARDEN, IN THE KEW ARBORETUM.

Ready for a new century

The addition of the wings gave the Temperate House the outline we are familiar with today but visually it looked quite different at the turn of the century. The central block and octagons were still glazed in green glass, while the new wings had clear glass. The exterior, which previously may not have been painted at all, was stone-coloured rather than brilliant white. Internally, a white

above: Himalaya House — north wing.

and green paint was used throughout but the shades varied: the wings were dark bronzish whereas the central block (and probably octagons) were a bluish mid-green.

With its wings in place, the Temperate House's five linked pavilions stretched 191 m with an internal area of 4,880 sq m, making it world's largest Victorian-era ornamental glasshouse. The opening of the north wing in 1899 marked its completion, 40 years after Burton's first designs and 36 years after the central block's opening: a period of construction that outlasted the lives of the three men most closely associated with the project.

left: Mexican House — south wing.

FROM IMPERIAL BOTANY TO CONSERVATION SCIENCE

A glasshouse fit for Empire

Lindley's vision for Kew, set out in the late 1830s, was for a national garden at the heart of the imperial endeavour. The wealth of the Empire depended on plants for agriculture, commerce and medicine, and by the dawn of the twentieth century nowhere at Kew better represented this than the Temperate House, with collections including such economically important plants as tea and cinchona, and representations of the flora of important colonies such as Australia, New Zealand and the Cape. William Hooker's annual reports reveal just how important the policy of aiding colonial industries was and if anything this activity increased still further under Joseph Hooker and Thiselton-Dyer. In 1898, Chamberlain informed Parliament 'I do not think it is too much to say that at the present time there are several of our important colonies, which owe whatever prosperity they possess to the knowledge and experience of, and the assistance given by the authorities at Kew'. A few years later, in 1902, Thiselton-Dyer gained official status at the Colonial Office as Botanical Adviser to the Secretary of State for the Colonies, a post maintained by successive Kew directors until 1941, albeit with declining influence.

Winds of change

In the decades following Second World War, as the Empire disintegrated and newly-independent nations struggled with difficult political, economic and environmental legacies, a different mood prevailed. Efforts to form an international organisation for nature protection pre-date First World War, but it was not until 1947 — the year of Indian independence and partition — that a provisional union was established. Formerly inaugurated as the IUPN the following year in 1956 it became the IUCN, the International Union for Conservation of Nature and Natural Resources (see box on p. 18).

As Britain's remaining colonies sped towards independence during the 1960s, a nascent environmental movement was on the rise, as awareness grew that human actions can have devastating environmental consequences. In the decades that have passed since, it has become clear that we are currently facing the greatest global challenges ever experienced by humankind. Climate change, habitat destruction, disease, population growth and the need to ensure food and fuel security are taking an unprecedented toll on Earth's natural resources.

Kew in the twenty-first century

Plants provide the food we eat, the clothes we wear, the medicines we take and the air we breathe. All our lives depend on plants. This simple but often overlooked truth guides Kew's scientific work today. Kew plays an important role in researching plant diversity and uses for humanity, working in 110 countries with over 400 collaborating institutions worldwide. This scientific knowledge, coupled with evidence-based global actions, is helping conserve the extraordinary diversity of plants on Earth and working towards possible solutions for the global environmental challenges facing humanity. Kew's work and its collections have never been more vital.

In 2000 Kew's Millennium Seed Bank (MSB) opened at Wakehurst. Seed banks such as the MSB provide an insurance policy against the extinction of plants in the wild. The Kew-led Millennium Seed Bank Partnership, the world's most extensive partnership for conserving the seeds of wild plants, already contains over two billion seeds from more than 37,000 species and is working to conserve 25% of the world's bankable species by 2020, prioritising threatened and useful plants.

View down Pagoda Vista, with Temperate House (left), Pavilion tea room (right), and Palm House in the distance, c. 1900–1910.

KEW'S ROLE IN CITES, THE CBD AND THE GSPC

The Convention on International Trade in Endangered Species of Wild Fauna and Flora (CITES) came into force internationally in 1976. Currently there are 183 Parties to the Convention. Each country that has signed up provides a Scientific Authority — Kew is the UK's Scientific Authority for CITES.

The Convention on Biological Diversity (CBD) came into force in 1993 with three objectives: to conserve biodiversity, ensure sustainable use, and ensure fair and equitable sharing of benefits from uses of genetic resources. Today there are 199 parties to the convention. Kew 's work provides the scientific evidence to underpin and inform global policy decisions relating to the CBD. In 2002 the CBD initiated the Global Strategy for Plant Conservation (GSPC). Sixteen targets are in place for 2020, with Kew actively contributing to many of them.

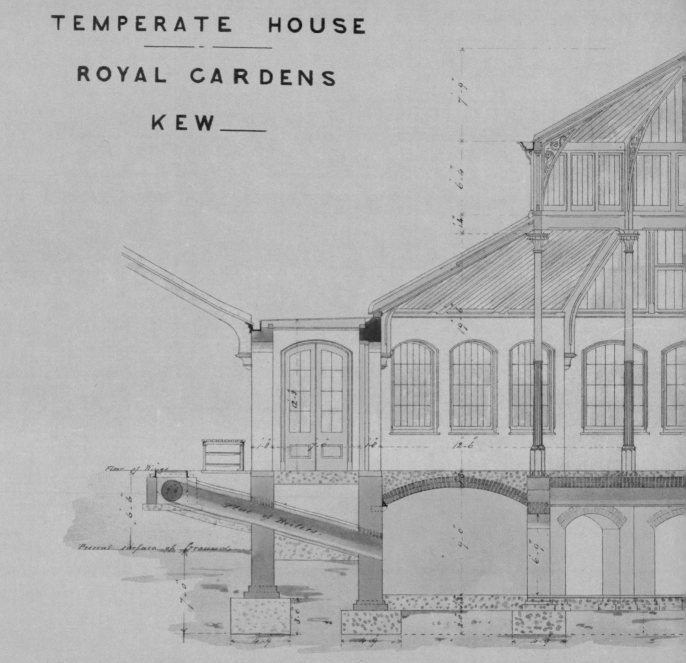

TEMPERATE HOUSE

ROYAL GARDENS

KEW___

Floor of Wings.

Plan of Boilers.

Present surface of Ground.

LONGITUDINAL

SECTION OF OCTAGONS_

Flue of Centre

Flue of Boilers

Present surface of Ground

Decimus Burton
6 Spring Garden
6 Decr 1859

20 feet.

EXPLORING THE PLANT COLLECTION

Asia

Rice paper plant

Tetrapanax papyrifer has been in the Temperate House since at least 1867 and still grows there today. Commonly known as the rice paper plant, it is the source of pith, a material favoured by Chinese artists during the nineteenth century for the vibrancy it lends to watercolours. These paintings, traditionally depicting scenes of everyday life, birds, or flowers, became popular with travellers looking for souvenirs. Back in Europe botanists quickly realised the material used for these paintings was not paper, but the plant it came from was unknown in the west until William Hooker named it in 1852.

The *Kew Guide* for 1867 provides an account of the pith-making process from John Bowring, Consul at Canton from the late 1840s to early 1850s, who donated many pith-related items to Kew (now in the Economic Botany Collection). First the cut stems were soaked for several days to loosen the surrounding bark and wood. When the core of pith had been removed it was cut into cylindrical lengths. A knife would then be run around the edge while the cylinder was being turned, to plane off thin, even, slices.

Rather than sinking into the material, as paint sinks into paper, thick applications of paint sit on this smooth surface, creating an embossed and luminous appearance. Unfortunately, as pith ages it becomes brittle and splits easily, and conservation is challenging as pith can expand and contract dramatically with wetting and drying. One conservator experienced in the medium is Eleanor Hasler, who adapted paper conservation techniques to conserve an album of paintings originally belonging to Dr Nathaniel Bagshaw Ward, inventor of the Wardian case, which was presented to Kew in 1964. Working on a light box and

Tetrapanax papyrifer by W. H. Fitch, 1852.

using the minimum amount of moisture to apply adhesive and Japanese repair tissue, she was able to mend tears in the fragile paintings. The traditional visual appearance of ribbon mounting was recreated using Japanese paper to secure the paintings with ribbon stretched across on top, giving the pith the ability to expand and flex as necessary.

Himalayan rhododendrons

Before the addition of the north and south wings, two of the Temp erate House's 20 beds were dedicated to rhododendrons, with one specifically for rhododendrons from the Himalaya. Many of the specimens displayed were discovered by Joseph Hooker during his expedition to India from 1847 to 1851 and published in his magnificent *Rhododendrons of the Sikkim Himalaya*. When naming new species, Hooker often chose to honour the friends, botanists and patrons of science who helped his expedition. *Rhododendron falconeri* is one example, named after Hugh Falconer, the botanist and geologist who succeeded Nathaniel Wallich as superintendent at Calcutta Botanic Garden. He was instrumental in Hooker's decision to travel to India, and the Himalaya specifically. In the preface to his *Himalayan Journals* Hooker tells us that his choice 'lay between India and the Andes, and I decided upon the former, being principally influenced by Dr Falconer . . . he drew my attention to the fact that we were ignorant even of the geography of the central and eastern parts of these mountains, while all the north was involved in a mystery equally attractive to the traveller and the naturalist.'

Another example is *R. campbelliae* named in honour of the wife of Archibald Campbell, superintendent of Darjeeling with whom Hooker travelled into Sikkim, a small impoverished state that shared borders with Tibet, Nepal and Bhutan, ruled by an elderly rajah. When the pair, already unwanted guests in the state, knowingly violated the Tibet border in November 1849, they were

Rhododendron maddenii, from J. D. Hooker's *Rhododendrons of Sikkim Himalaya*.

Rhododendron falconeri by Marianne North.

Rhododendron ciliatum by W. H. Fitch, 1851.

arrested and imprisoned. The British government secured their release by threatening to send an invasion force and the rajah was severely, arguably excessively, punished by the annexation of some of his land and the withdrawal of his British pension.

When the north wing of the Temperate House was added in the 1890s the rhododendrons in the central block were moved there, and supplemented with many additional specimens. Bean, writing in 1908, saw rhododendrons as 'the predominant feature' of the wing, 'flowering during the first five months of the year and ranging in colour from blood-red through all the grades of rose and pink, to white.'

Today *R. falconeri* and *R. campbelliae* (now named *R. arboretum* var. *cinnamomeum*) and some other Himalayan rhododendrons are grown outside at Kew. *R. maddenii*, named for 'a good and accomplished botanist', Major Madden of the Bengal Civil Service, and *R. ciliatum* — both displayed in the early Temperate House — are part of the glasshouse's current collection, which comprises some 25 species from many regions.

Rhododendron campbellie by W. H. Fitch, 1849.

THE IUCN
INTERNATIONAL UNION FOR CONSERVATION OF NATURE
The IUCN Red List of Threatened Species classifies the conservation status of plants, fungi and animal species. Quantitative criteria are used to asses a species as one of the following: Extinct, Extinct in the Wild, Critically Endangered, Endangered, Vulnerable, Near Threatened and Least Concern. Species not yet evaluated are listed as Not Evaluated and those where there is inadequate information to make an assessment are listed as Data Deficient. These classifications play an important role in guiding conservation activities of governments, NGOs and scientists across the world. Kew has a Red List Partnership agreement with the IUCN, and our staff contribute many hundreds of hours each year to the red-listing process. Many plants in the Temperate House are IUCN listed.

Africa

Wood's cycad

IUCN status: Extinct in the Wild

The Temperate House's Wood's cycad (*Encephalartos woodii*) is an offset of the only plant of this species ever found in the wild. It was sent to Kew in 1899, four years after John Medley Wood (1827–1915) discovered the lone male plant growing on the fringes of the Ngoye Forest. A passionate naturalist who immigrated to South Africa in 1852, Medley Wood managed Durban Botanic Garden from 1882 and established the Natal Herbarium (originally the Colonial Herbarium). His Kew-trained assistant James Wylie returned to the *E. woodii* plant in 1903 to collect smaller offsets, and four years later returned to collect two of the larger stems (these still grow on the terrace at Durban today). That left the cycad with just two stems, one of which had died by 1912. The final stem was removed by the Forestry department in 1916, rendering the tree extinct in the wild.

We do not know what drove *E. woodii* to extinction, or even if it was ever more widespread. The area it was found in has been well-explored but not thoroughly surveyed so there is still hope that a female plant may be found that could reproduce with male clones, which number around 500 worldwide. A project is underway which aims to eventually produce a 'pure' female by cross-breeding *E. woodii* clones with the genetically closely-related species *E. natalensis*, and then successively backcrossing the resulting female hybrid offspring with male *E. woodii* specimens.

John Medley Wood stands next to a specimen of *Encephalartos woodii* (Wood's cycad) in the Durban Botanic Gardens. From *Kew Bulletin*, 1914.

Bird of paradise flower

The South African genus *Strelitzia*, commonly known as bird of paradise flower, was introduced to Europe in 1773 by Kew's earliest plant collector, Francis Masson. Joseph Banks named the genus in honour of King George III's wife Queen Charlotte the Duchess of Mecklenburg-Strelitz, who lived at Kew for many years. *Strelitzia reginae,* with its striking beautifully-coloured flowers, has been grown at Kew ever since and was the first plant to be placed in the Temperate House's south wing after its 1970s restoration.

above: *Strelitzia augusta*, South Africa, by Marianne North.

When it opened in the 1860s, it was not *S. reginae* but the white-flowered *S. augusta* (now *S. alba*) that graced the Temperate House beds. This species was also introduced by Masson, in the 1790s, and it is the rarest *Strelitzia* species. When the wings were added in the 1890s another *Strelitzia* species — the blue-and-white-flowered *S. nicolai*, named after the Russian emperor Nicolas I — was planted in the south wing and the other *Strelitzia* specimens moved there. In 1908 Bean wrote that the strelitzias were 'very striking', *S. reginae* for its orange and blue flowers, *S. augusta* for its height, and *S. nicolai* for its splendid leaves. All three species can still be seen in the glasshouse today

left: *Strelitzia reginae* and sugar birds, South Africa, by Marianne North.

Australia and New Zealand

Tree ferns

The tree ferns *Dicksonia antarcticum*, native to Australia and rare in New Zealand, and *Dicksonia squarrosa*, native to New Zealand, have been a popular feature of the Temperate House since it first opened. In the original 1860s planting arrangement, they featured in four of the twenty beds. Prior to this the ferns and other iconic Australasian plants such as kauri trees (*Agathis* species) suffered by being grown in an overcrowded palm stove that William Hooker declared 'old and worthless'.

Undoubtedly attractive, especially when their large spreading crowns are viewed from above, they are also robust. The government botanist of Victoria, Baron von Mueller, reported that *B. antarcticum* survived the long sea voyage between Australia and Europe best, stating that 'a fresh frondless stem, even if weighing nearly half a ton, requires only to be placed without any packing in the hold of a vessel as ordinary goods, to secure its safe arrival in Europe, the vitality being fully thus retained for several months, particularly if the stem is occasionally moistened.'

The trunk of tree ferns are formed from a slender stem surrounded by fibrous roots. They are slow growers, taking over 20 years to reach maturity but can grow to form an extremely thick trunk and obtain a height of up to 15 metres. It is possible for their trunks to divide by producing offsets, although this is rare: one correspondent of Hooker's in the 1860 was so taken with a multi-stemmed tree fern he saw in Tasmania that he declared himself 'satisfied it is one of the wonders of the world.' The genus name honours James Dickson (1738—1822) a Scottish

Tree ferns in the Temperate House, c. 1900–1910.

botanist, gardener and nurseryman who through a personal recommendation from Joseph Banks became gardener at the British Museum in 1781. Dickson went on to play a role in the founding of two great institutions: the Linnean Society in 1788 and the Horticultural Society (now Royal Horticultural Society), where he served as vice-president.

Bunya pine

The bunya pine (*Araucaria bidwillii*) was named by William Hooker in 1843. The genus name is derived from the tribe name 'Aracanos', while the species epithet honours its collector, the botanist John Bidwill, who sent specimens from Australia to Kew for identification. Before finding their home in the Temperate House's central block in the 1860s, Kew's specimens were grown in the Orangery and an old greenhouse earmarked for demolition. Evidently the bunya pines grew well in their new home as in the 1890s the *Garden and Forest* journal reported that they almost reached the roof. Presumably they touched it soon after, as by the time Bean wrote about them in 1908 they had been reduced in height several times. In the wild the tree can grow to 35 m and produces large cones which can weight up to 10 kg.

Native to south-eastern Queensland, the bunya pine has great significance to Aboriginal people, for whom it is sacred. Its edible nuts, which have an almond-like flavour and are still eaten today, were historically important as a ceremonial food during bunya gatherings. Thousands of people would gather for these events which lasted for months and involved discussions, negotiations and settlements over legal, marriage and regional issues.

Initially a Crown decree issued by the Governor in 1842 protected these important native trees, but this was rescinded by an Act in 1860 and for the following half a century the trees were felled for timber. By the early years of the twentieth century concern over their fate led to the creation of the Bunya Mountains National Park in 1908. Today, despite significant historic exploitation, the species is not threatened. However maintaining existing wild populations is a priority for Australian conservation organisations due to the trees continuing importance for indigenous groups and as it is predicted to be negatively affected by climate change.

Kōwhai

Kōwhai is the common name for the eight *Sophora* species endemic to New Zealand. The kōwhai species *Sophora tetraptera* has resided in the Temperate House since the 1860s and has been grown at Kew since at least 1789 after being brought to Europe by Joseph Banks, who collected it during the *Endeavour* voyage (1768–71).

Seed was planted in the Apothecaries Garden at Chelsea (now Chelsea Physic Garden) during the 1770s. The tree it grew into was illustrated for *Curtis's Botanical Magazine* in 1792 — one of the first coloured illustrations of a native New Zealand plant. It is depicted thickly covered with the flowers it is famed for: 'A finer sight can scarcely be imagined', writes the author of the description, '...they have a peculiar richness, which is impossible to represent in colouring'. It is this colour that accounts for the common name 'kōwhai', the Māori word for yellow. The showy clusters of golden drooping blooms are New Zealand's unofficial national flower, loved by many. Its arrival in the late winter is said to mark the season's last frost.

Kōwhai was an important medicinal tree for the Māoris. Poultices made from the crushed bark and leaves steeped in water were used to treat a wide array of skin conditions and to dress wounds,

Araucaria bidwillii, Australia, by Marianne North, c. 1980.

cuts, bruises and broken bones. Perhaps its most famous use was in 1925 when George Nepia, a famous player for the All Blacks rugby team, opted for a kōwhai remedy instead of surgery after bursting a blood vessel in his leg during play. The treatment was so successful he was back on the field the following week. While there are records of it being used as an infusion drunk for colds and sore throats ingestion is not advised as many parts of the plant, and especially its yellow seeds, contain toxic alkaloids.

Sophora tetraptera by
Sydenham Edwards, from *The
Botanical Magazine*, 1791.

The Americas

Chilean wine palm

IUCN status: Vulnerable

Bean wrote that the Temperate House's Chilean wine palm
(*Jubaea chilensis*) was 'the most remarkable palm in the house'.
The tree he would have seen in 1908 was the famous specimen
raised from seed in the 1840s that resided in the Temperate
House, thrusting up towards the roof, until the house closed for
restoration in 2013. By then that grand individual, possibly the
world's tallest glasshouse plant, had outgrown the space available
and sadly was too big to move — however, seed was saved from
it and numerous young plants have now been grown.

Darwin was no fan of the palm's distinctive appearance. He
described the trees he saw when the *Beagle* reached Chile in
August 1834 as being 'for their family, ugly trees. Their stem is
very large, and of a curious form, being thicker in the middle than
at base or top.' He went on to describe the process by which
sap was extracted: 'Every year in the early spring, in August, very
many are cut down, and when the trunk is lying on the ground,
the crown of leaves is lopped off. The sap then immediately
begins to flow from the upper end, and continues so doing for
some months; it is, however, necessary that a thin slice should be
shaved off from that end every morning, so as to expose a fresh
surface.' Historically abundant, over-harvesting for this sap (which
is reduced to make the sweet syrup known as palm honey) has
greatly reduced populations. Under Chilean law harvesting is now
limited and local conservation groups are attempting to reforest
areas within the palm's natural range.

Jubaea chilensis, Chile, by Marianne North, c. 1884.

Mexican hand tree

The bizarre looking and aptly named Mexican hand tree (*Chiranthodendron pentadactylon*) — also known by the evocative name devil's hand tree on account of its flower resembling a scarlet clawed-hand — has been grown at Kew since at least the 1840s, and has lived in the Temperate House since the 1860s.

The explorer and naturalist Alexander von Humboldt saw the plant in Mexico c.1801, where it had long been venerated. He recorded that 'one solitary individual existed in the whole Mexican Confederation — one ancient stock of this marvellous plant. It was believed that the tree had been planted 500 years before by a king of Toluca, as a specimen of exotic vegetation.' Humboldt and his travelling companion Aimè Bonpland, a French botanist and explorer took seeds back to Paris but none germinated. Further seeds were obtained and by 1811 the plant featured in botanical collections in Paris and Montpellier — soon afterwards it was introduced to England and it is likely Kew's first specimen dated from this time.

The Mexican hand tree is popular in cultivation but its native cloud forest habitat is threatened by extremely high deforestation rates, and may face further threat from climate change. The tree has not yet been evaluated for the global Red List but is classified as Vulnerable in The Red List of Mexican Cloud Forest Trees.

Mexican hand tree, by W. H. Fitch, from *Curtis's Botanical Magazine*, 1859.

Islands

St Helena redwood

IUCN status: Extinct in the Wild

The St Helena redwood (*Trochetiopsis erythroxylon*) in the Temperate House has been grown from seed collected from the last wild tree, which died in the 1950s. It was first cultivated at Kew around 1800 with repeated attempts to raise healthy young plants made during the Temperate House's early decades.

St Helena, a small island in the Atlantic Ocean, has just one percent of its native forest remaining — despite being entirely covered in vegetation when discovered by the Portuguese in 1502. Its redwood first reached Europe thanks to Joseph Banks, who took specimens to Kew following his short visit in 1771. Banks decided the island was ideally suited for crop growing and as a temporary respite home for plants undergoing long sea voyages, noting it to be 'situated in a degree between temperate and warm their soil might produce most if not all the vegetables of Europe together with the fruit of the Indies'. Before long, the island's native flora, already in decline due to goats introduced by the Portuguese, faced a different threat: the indiscriminate wide-scale introduction of plants deemed potentially useful for British Colonies.

In 1805 William Burchell arrived in St Helena, initially to act as schoolmaster. By this time such introductions, coupled with unmitigated felling and clearing, had ravaged the island: his journal notes 'the decayed remains of trees and shrubs which must formerly have covered all these hills'. Later appointed the British East India Company's naturalist on the island, Burchell's observations over five years provided a benchmark for the island's indigenous flora, although his findings were unknown until after his death in 1863, when his sister presented his botanical collections to Kew.

Burchell's papers suggest the redwood was reasonably plentiful at the start of the nineteenth century; but by the 1870s John Charles Melliss, an engineer and amateur naturalist resident on the island, recorded the redwood as 'quickly disappearing, and ere long will probably become altogether extinct . . . altogether not more than seventeen or eighteen plants are now to be found on the island', in his book *St Helena, A Physical, Historical and Topographical Description of the Island* (1875). Kew's Daniel Morris visited in 1883 and brought back seed from which plants were raised — but they did not fare well and the last few died during the winter of

Archway, St Helena, from William Burchell's sketchbooks, 1805.

1891. Subsequent attempts have proved just how challenging the redwood is to cultivate and reintroduce to the wild. Historically a timber tree growing up to eight metres, the cultivated specimens of today lack the vigour of their wild counterpart and only grow to half this height. The c.60 specimens existing today suffer inbreeding depression and have a severely limited gene pool, as all are derived from the last wild tree.

CONSERVING ST HELENA'S FLORA

In 1991 the Overseas Development Administration funded a Sustainable Environment and Development Strategy for St Helena with Kew as an advisor on habitat conservation and propagation of rare endemics. Kew's staff play an important role in efforts to conserve St Helena's flora today, undertaking botanical surveys, collecting and banking seed, and providing training and support to conservationists based on the island. A Darwin Initiative grant supports its work with the St Helena government to ensure their extremely threatened flora is better represented in seed bank collections on the island and at the MSB. With ten endemic species currently represented by fewer than 100 wild individuals, the race is on to save species through propagation, habitat restoration and reintroduction.

Kew's work on St Helena exemplifies its wider aims and practices, working in collaboration with governments and institutions across the globe to understand and conserve Earth's incredible — and vital — plant diversity.

Trochetiopsis erythroxylon from William Burchell's sketchbooks, 1809.

FURTHER READING

Brockway, L. (2002). *Science and Colonial Expansion: the role of the British Royal Botanic Gardens*. Reprint. Yale University Press. New Haven & London.

Desmond, R. (2007). *The History of Kew*. 2nd ed. Royal Botanic Gardens, Kew.

Fry, C. (2009). *The Plant Hunters*. Andre Deutsch. London.

Grant, F. (2013). *Glasshouses*. Shire Publications. Oxford.

Griggs, P. (2011). *Joseph Hooker: botanical trailblazer*. Royal Botanic Gardens, Kew.

Hooker, J. (2017). *Joseph Hooker's Rhododendrons of Sikkim-Himalaya*. Royal Botanic Gardens, Kew.

Monem, N. (ed.) (2007). *Botanic Gardens: a living history* Black Dog. London.

Payne, M. (2016). *Marianne North: a very intrepid painter*, revised ed. Royal Botanic Gardens, Kew.

Willis, K. and Fry, C. (2014). *Plants from Roots to Riches*. John Murray. London.

Online Resources

Critical Ecosystem Partnership Fund http://www.cepf.net

IUCN Red List http://www.iucnredlist.org

Millennium Ecosystem Assessment https://www.millenniumassessment.org/en/index.html

Plants of the World Online http://www.plantsoftheworldonline.org

State of the World's Plants https://stateoftheworldsplants.com

Acknowledgements

The author would like to thank Gina Fullerlove, Lydia White, Georgina Hills and Christina Harrison from Kew Publishing, Sharon Willoughby and Alison Foster from the Interpretation team, and Francesca Mackenzie from Library Art and Archives.

Kew Publishing would like to thank Julia Buckley, Colin Clubbe, Dave Cooke, Georgina Darroch, Aerial Finch, Mark Nesbitt, Lynn Parker, Scott Taylor, Tracy Wells and Richard Wilford.

First published in 2018
Royal Botanic Gardens, Kew, Richmond, Surrey, TW9 3AB, UK   www.kew.org

ISBN 978-1-84246-664-3

British Library Cataloguing in Publication Data
A catalogue record for this book is available from the British Library.

Text: Michelle Payne
Design and page layout: Christine Beard
Production manager: Georgina Hills
Cover design illustration: Donald Insall Associates
Central fold-out pages: Original drawings for the Temperate House by Decimus Burton, 1859 (outside); planting plan for the restored Temperate House, 2018 (inside).

Printed in the UK by L & S Printing Company Limited

The paper used for this publication is FSC certified

For information or to purchase all Kew titles please visit shop.kew.org/kewbooksonline or email publishing@kew.org

Kew's mission is to be the global resource in plant and fungal knowledge and the world's leading botanic garden.

Kew receives about half of its running costs from Government through the Department for Environment, Food and Rural Affairs (Defra). All other funding needed to support Kew's vital work comes from members, foundations, donors and commercial activities, including book sales